司馬光

Heroes and Role Models | Non-Fiction Series

Copyright © 2022 by Level Learning, INC. and Washington Yu Ying PCS™
Original and Edited Text Copyright © 2022 by Washington Yu Ying PCS™

All rights reserved. No part of this book in whole or part may be reproduced without written permission from the publisher.

Published by Level Learning, INC.

Content Contributors:
Washington Yu Ying PCS™
Level Learning - Ya-Ching Chang

Illustrations by: Josh Taira

Leveling classification based on Level Learning standard. For full description, visit www.levellearning.com

ISBN 978-1-64040-039-9
Traditional Chinese Edition

About Level Learning:

Level Learning provides a literacy focused curriculum specifically designed for K-12 Chinese as a Second Language classrooms. Our program offers 20 levels of specific and detailed objectives, leveled texts and passages, mastery-based online assessment, and analytics to enable data-driven instruction. Level Learning reading curriculum for both literature and informational text emphasize grammar and comprehension skills to help teachers develop confident and independent Chinese language readers. The non-fiction series of books are specifically designed to support our informational text course based on multiple national standards. To learn more about our entire offering, visit www.levellearning.com.

About Washington Yu Ying PCS™:

Washington Yu Ying PCS is a Mandarin English dual language immersion International Baccalaureate (IB) World school. Yu Ying's mission is to inspire and prepare young people to create a better world by challenging them to reach their full potential in a nurturing Chinese/English educational environment. Yu Ying's comprehensive IB, dual immersion curriculum equips students with global competencies for success in the real world. As a leader in immersion education, Yu Ying is determined to advance Chinese language programs and global citizenry education by helping other schools create and strengthen their Chinese programs. For more information, email: products@washingtonyuying.org

司馬光，宋朝人，出生於1019年。他是中國古代著名的歷史學家。

司馬光從小就對歷史非常感興趣,在他的書架上經常放滿了許多跟歷史有關的圖書。他每天都會花很長時間閱讀這些書。

司馬光非常聰明，遇到難題時喜歡思考，找到解決問題的辦法。在他小時候，有一次他和朋友們一起在院子裡玩，突然一個朋友不小心掉進了水缸裡。其他的孩子都嚇得大哭，不知道該怎麼辦。

只有司馬光沒有哭,他冷靜地用石頭砸破水缸。就這樣,掉進去的孩子被救了出來。

長大以後,司馬光還是認真努力地學習歷史,把自己的才能用到和歷史有關的事情上。

《資治通鑑》是司馬光寫的一套非常有名的歷史書。這套書裡講了16個朝代，一共1362年的歷史。

在編這套書的時候，司馬光經常忙得忘記吃飯，很晚才睡覺。每次遇到難題，他都會努力地找出答案。

因為司馬光做事認真,他花了十九年的時間,才終於完成了這套書。直到現在,《資治通鑑》在中國的歷史書中都有著非常重要的地位。

Glossary

	Pinyin	English Definition
宋朝	sòng cháo	Song dynasty
著名	zhù míng	famous
歷史學家	lì shǐ xué jiā	historian
歷史	lì shǐ	history
興趣	xìng qù	interest
書架	shū jià	bookshelf
有關	yǒu guān	related
書	shū	books
閱讀	yuè dú	to read
聰明	cōng míng	smart, intelligent
難題	nán tí	problem
思考	sī kǎo	to think, to reflect
解決	jiě jué	to solve
突然	tū rán	suddenly
水缸	shuǐ gāng	water tank

	Pinyin	English Definition
嚇	xià	scared
冷靜	lěng jìng	calm, cool
砸破	zá pò	smash
救	jiù	to save
認真	rèn zhēn	serious
努力	nǔ lì	hardworking
才能	cái néng	talent
一套	yí tào	a set, a series
朝代	cháo dài	dynasty
忘記	wàng jì	to forget
答案	dá àn	answer
終於	zhōng yú	finally
完成	wán chéng	to complete
地位	dì wèi	rank, place

www.ingramcontent.com/pod-product-compliance
Lightning Source LLC
Chambersburg PA
CBHW041224070526
44584CB00001B/84